FTCE

Middle Grades General Science 5-9 Practice Questions

DEAR FUTURE EXAM SUCCESS STORY

First of all, **THANK YOU** for purchasing Mometrix study materials!

Second, congratulations! You are one of the few determined test-takers who are committed to doing whatever it takes to excel on your exam. **You have come to the right place.** We developed these practice tests with one goal in mind: to deliver you the best possible approximation of the questions you will see on test day.

Standardized testing is one of the biggest obstacles on your road to success, which only increases the importance of doing well in the high-pressure, high-stakes environment of test day. Your results on this test could have a significant impact on your future, and these practice tests will give you the repetitions you need to build your familiarity and confidence with the test content and format to help you achieve your full potential on test day.

Your success is our success

We would love to hear from you! If you would like to share the story of your exam success or if you have any questions or comments in regard to our products, please contact us at **800-673-8175** or **support@mometrix.com**.

Thanks again for your business and we wish you continued success!

Sincerely,
The Mometrix Test Preparation Team

Printed in the United States of America

TABLE OF CONTENTS

Practice Test #1

1. Which of the following statements correctly describes the relationship between temperature and density in water?

a. As the temperature of liquid water decreases, density decreases monotonically.
b. As the temperature of frozen water (ice) increases, density decreases monotonically.
c. Water in the solid state generally has a higher density than water in the liquid state.
d. Water in the liquid state generally has a higher density than water in the solid state.

2. Why would it be ethical for local and state governments to conduct a risk-benefit analysis in making decisions about city planning and development?

a. Governments must know what the benefits of a new development are for people and the economy in order to persuade opponents and the public who are against it.
b. Knowledge of the environmental risks and benefits to humans is required for gaining building permits.
c. The benefits to people and the economy must outweigh the risks to determine whether their decision to build is fair.
d. The benefits to people and the economy can be used to ignore the risks associated with any new development.

3. Why is it important to form a hypothesis before performing an experiment?

a. The experimenter will not have enough time to create a hypothesis after beginning the experiment
b. Developing a hypothesis ensures that the lab will be safe
c. The experiment will take too much time to complete if there is no hypothesis
d. The hypothesis tells what the experiment is going to be testing

4. Two waves, each of which has an amplitude of A, cross paths. At the point where they cross, the peak of one wave meets the trough of another wave. What is the resulting amplitude at the point where the waves cross?

a. 0
b. A
c. $2A$
d. $-A$

5. Proteins are made up of repeating subunits of which of the following?

a. Sugars
b. Triglycerides
c. Amino acids
d. Nucleic acids

6. Which of the following statements about radioactive decay is true?

a. The sum of the mass of the daughter particles is less than that of the parent nucleus.
b. The sum of the mass of the daughter particles is greater than that of the parent nucleus.
c. The sum of the mass of the daughter particles is equal to that of the parent nucleus.
d. The sum of the mass of the daughter particles cannot be accurately measured.

7. Which of the following is NOT an effect on the environment due to deforestation?

a. Loss of biodiversity
b. Soil erosion
c. Decrease in carbon dioxide in atmosphere
d. Disruptions in the water cycle

8. Which of the following is a disadvantage of biomass energy?

a. Using it releases a lot of carbon.
b. It is non-renewable.
c. It requires a lot of space.
d. Current processes require rare earth metals to utilize the energy.

Refer to the following for question 9:

After a laboratory experiment that involved using various chemical solutions, you and your lab partner are asked to clean up your workspace. The teacher states that any chemicals that have been poured into a new container should be disposed of, but the chemicals still in their original bottles can be placed into storage.

9. Which of the following is NOT a recommended storage practice for laboratory chemicals?

a. Chemicals should be stored at the appropriate temperature and humidity.
b. Chemicals should be dated when received and when opened.
c. Chemicals may be routinely stored on bench tops.
d. Chemicals should be stored on shelves with raised outer edges.

10. Which of the following describes the correct short-term storage method for liquid-filled pH probes?

a. Store the pH probes in distilled water.
b. Store the pH probes on a dry shelf.
c. Store the pH probes in a potassium chloride solution.
d. Store the pH probes in hydrochloric acid.

11. Which of the atomic models listed below is the most recent?

a. Rutherford's atomic model
b. Bohr's atomic model
c. Thomson's atomic model
d. Dalton's atomic model

12. A virus that has been incorporated into the DNA of its host is called a:

a. Lysogenic cycle
b. Lytic cycle
c. Retrovirus
d. Provirus

13. Which of the following statements correctly describes a difference between the lithosphere and the asthenosphere?

a. The asthenosphere is composed of atmospheric gas, while the lithosphere is composed of liquids and solids.
b. The asthenosphere is hotter and more fluid than the lithosphere.
c. The lithosphere is hotter and has a different chemical composition than the asthenosphere.
d. Heat is transferred through conduction in the asthenosphere, while it is transferred through convection in the lithosphere.

14. You blow up a rubber balloon and hold the opening tight with your fingers. You then release your fingers, causing air to blow out of the balloon. This pushes the balloon forward, causing the balloon to shoot across the room. Which of Newton's laws best explains the cause of this motion?

a. Newton's First Law
b. Newton's Second Law
c. Newton's Third Law
d. Newton's Fourth Law

15. Which of the following does NOT display an appropriate or safe use of chemicals?

a. Never taste any chemicals.
b. To test odors, waft the odors towards your nose with a cupped hand.
c. Never return unused chemicals to the stock bottle.
d. When diluting acids, always pour the water into the acid.

16. Describe the correct outer shell electronic arrangement of phosphorous.

a. $4s^2 4p^3$
b. $3s^2 3p^3$
c. $2s^2 3p^3$
d. $2s^2 2p^3$

17. Which of the following is NOT an impact of strip mining of coal?

a. Destruction of landscapes, forest, and wildlife habitats
b. Dust and noise pollution
c. Chemical contamination of groundwater
d. Lowering of the water table

18. A 4-kilogram bowling ball moving at 10 meters per second hits a stationary 1-kilogram bowling ball in a head-on elastic collision. What is the speed of the stationary ball after the collision?

a. 0 m/s
b. 10 m/s
c. Less than 10 m/s, but not 0 m/s
d. More than 10 m/s

19. Three liquids, X, Y and Z are placed in separate flasks, each of which is suspended in a water bath at 75 °C. The boiling points of each liquid are

X, 273 K
Y, 340 K
Z, 360 K

Which of the three liquids will begin to boil after warming to 75 °C?

a. X, Y, and Z
b. X and Z
c. X and Y
d. Y and Z

20. Which of the following numbers has the most significant digits?

a. 1,500,000
b. 1.5000×10^5
c. 0.15000
d. 0.00150000

21. A 10-kg plastic block is at rest on a flat wooden surface. The coefficient of static friction between wood and plastic is 0.6, and the coefficient of kinetic friction is 0.5. How much horizontal force is needed to start the plastic box moving?

a. 5 N
b. 49 N
c. 59 N
d. 98 N

22. Who proposed the quantum theory of light?

a. James Maxwell
b. Christiaan Huygens
c. Isaac Newton
d. Albert Einstein

23. You throw a baseball straight up near the surface of Earth and it falls back to the ground. Which statement is true about the acceleration of the baseball at the top of its path? (Ignore air resistance.)

a. The acceleration is zero.
b. The acceleration changes sign.
c. The acceleration is $-9.8\ m/s^2$.
d. The acceleration continues to increase.

24. Four windows are washed with different cleaners. The same paper towel is used on each. The squares below show each window before being cleaned. What is the variable in the experiment?

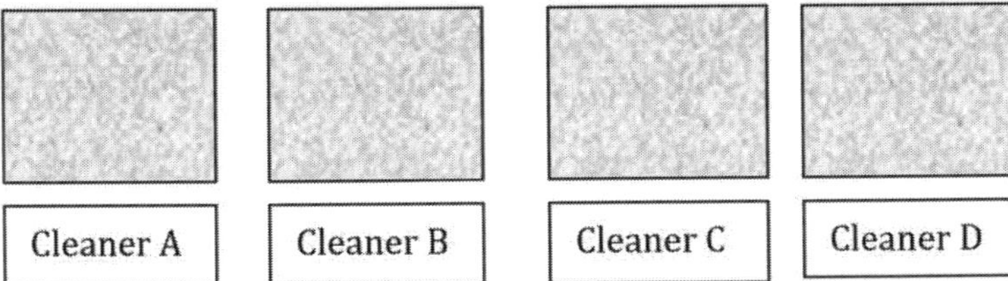

a. The amount of sunlight coming through the windows
b. The type of window cleaner used
c. The amount of dirt on each window
d. The type of paper towel used

25. In 1912, Alfred Wegener proposed a theory often referred to as "the Pangaea Theory." This theory was based on which of the following ideas?

a. The Earth's magnetic poles have reversed several times throughout history.
b. Tectonic plates move because of convection currents in the mantle.
c. Mountains are formed by tectonic plates pushing against one another.
d. The continents once formed a single land mass, but have since drifted apart.

26. The best way to separate isotopes of the same element is to exploit:

a. Differences in chemical reactivity
b. Differences in reduction potential
c. Differences in toxicity
d. Differences in mass

27. Which of the following is an example of the alternation of generations life cycle?

a. Asexual reproduction of strawberries by runners
b. Annual plants that live through a single growing season
c. Ferns that have a large diploid and a diminutive haploid stage
d. Insects that have distinct larval and adult stages

28. Transfer of DNA between bacteria using a narrow tube called a pilus is known as:

a. Transformation
b. Transduction
c. Operation
d. Conjugation

29. Earth rotates on its axis every 24 hours and revolves around the Sun every 365 earth days. Mars revolves around the Sun every 687 earth days. What does a period 687 earth days represent in terms of Mars time?

a. One Martian day
b. One Martian year
c. One Martian season
d. One Martian month

30. The masses of four different objects, taken with different scales, were 23.04 g, 7.12 g, 0.0088 g, and 5.423 g. What is the total mass of all four objects to the proper number of decimal places?

a. 35.59180 g
b. 35.5918 g
c. 35.60 g
d. 35.59 g

31. Which of the following common household products is NOT correctly matched with the chemical associated with it?

a. Vinegar and acetic acid
b. Glass cleaner and sodium hypochlorite
c. Baking soda and sodium bicarbonate
d. Rubbing alcohol and isopropanol

32. Two cars driving in opposite directions collide. If you ignore friction and any other outside interactions, which of the following statements is always true?

a. The total momentum is conserved.
b. The sum of the potential and kinetic energy is conserved.
c. The total velocity of the cars is conserved.
d. The total impulse is conserved.

33. In ferns, the joining of egg and sperm produces a zygote, which will grow into the

a. Gametophyte
b. Sporophyte
c. Spore
d. Sporangium

34. Which of the following could be an end product of transcription?

a. rRNA
b. DNA
c. Protein
d. snRNP

35. Which of the following wastes may be suitable for sink or sewer disposal?

a. Acetic acid
b. Benzene
c. Acetone
d. Mercury

36. The data below was collected by repeating the same experiment four different times. What conclusion can be drawn based on the data shown?

Bicycle Obstacle Race

Student	Trial 1	Trial 2	Trial 3	Trial 4
Kayla	57.6 s	37.6 s	37.3 s	36.2 s
Carson	64.0 s	32.6 s	31.2 s	28.4 s
Jeremy	59.2 s	31.0 s	28.8 s	27.9 s
Rachel	61.3 s	42.6 s	39.5 s	39.0 s

a. The data was accurate in all four trials
b. The data in trials 2 through 4 is probably inaccurate
c. An error occurred in trial 1 that gave inaccurate data
d. The times in trial 4 are fastest because the students were tired

37. Place the following elements in order of decreasing electronegativity:

N, As, Bi, P, Sb

a. As > Bi > N > P > Sb
b. N > P > As > Sb > Bi
c. Bi > Sb > As > P > N
d. P > N > As > Sb > Bi

38. For what reason is repetition important to scientific inquiry?

a. It is the only way to prove that an experiment is reliable.
b. It adds to the number of statistics supporting the concept.
c. It assists the scientist in determining which data to consider.
d. It requires many groups of investigators working on a project.

39. Which of the following plant structures allows for gas exchange?

a. Xylem
b. Phloem
c. Cuticle
d. Stomata

40. Consider the following statements about Newton's law:

I. A newton is a fundamental unit.
II. Mass and acceleration are inversely related when the force is constant.
III. Newton's first law can be derived from Newton's second law.
IV. Newton's second law can be derived from the universal law of gravity.

Which of the statements are true?

a. I, II, and III.
b. II and III only.
c. III only.
d. None of them

41. A person walks 4 meters in a single direction. He or she then changes directions and walks an additional 9 meters. What is the total magnitude of the displacement of the person?

a. It is 13 meters.
b. It is always larger than 9 meters but less than 13 meters.
c. It is less than 13 meters and as small as 5 meters.
d. It is less than 5 meters.

42. Use the information in the table to determine what would happen to the mass and weight of a human if he or she were on Neptune.

Mass	Mass is the amount of matter there is. Mass only changes when matter is added or removed.
Weight	Weight is how much gravity pulls downward on an object. The more gravity there is, the more an object weighs.
Gravity on Earth: 9.8 m/s^2	Gravity on Neptune: 11.15 m/s^2

a. A person's mass and weight would increase on Neptune
b. A person's mass and weight would decrease on Neptune
c. A person's mass would increase, but weight would be unchanged
d. A person's mass would be unchanged, but weight would increase

43. Which of the following is NOT supported by Dalton's atomic theory of matter?

a. Differences in properties of elements are due to differences in the atoms of the elements.
b. Atoms of a particular element all have the same properties, such as size and mass.
c. Every element consists of tiny particles called atoms, which can be split into even smaller pieces.
d. Chemical processes result from the rearrangement, combination, and separation of atoms.

44. Which scientist was responsible for developing the format of the modern periodic table?

a. Faraday
b. Einstein
c. Hess
d. Mendeleev

45. Physical weathering of rocks can be caused by all of the following EXCEPT:

a. The freezing and thawing of water on the surface of rocks
b. Changes in temperature
c. Oxidation
d. Changes in pressure due to the removal of overlying rocks

46. The lithification process results in the formation of which of the following types of rocks?

a. Sedimentary
b. Intrusive igneous
c. Extrusive igneous
d. Metamorphic

47. An automobile increased its speed uniformly from 20 m/s to 30 m/s at rate 5 m/s^2. During this time, it traveled 50 meters. How long did it take the automobile to make this change?

a. 5 seconds
b. 2 seconds
c. 10 seconds
d. Can't be determined.

48. Resonance structures can be defined as:

a. Two or more structures that have different atoms bound to different atoms
b. Two structures that have a similar structure but different formula
c. Two or more structures that have the same formula, but are different in shape
d. Two or more structures that differ only in the arrangement of electrons in the structures

49. Minerals that form on the sea floor from discarded shells are most likely part of which chemical class?

a. Sulfate
b. Organic
c. Carbonate
d. Silicate

50. Which of the following types of igneous rock solidifies deepest beneath the Earth's surface?

a. Hypabyssal
b. Plutonic
c. Volcanic
d. Detrital

Refer to the following for question 51:

> Your class is competing with another class to determine who can produce the tallest plants. Your class decides to test a couple of solutions to determine which would be best for overall plant growth before competing. Starting with four sets of four plants, the class decides to water each set with a different solution. They water them once a week with 200ml of the following solutions: water, diet soda, 1% bleach solution, and a 1% salt solution. All plants are placed in the window that receives the recommended amount of light. After a month of testing, your class notices that only two plants are alive, but one of those two does not look healthy.

51. What is the control, if any, in this experiment?

a. There is no control in this experiment
b. The control is the water
c. The control is the diet soda
d. The control is the amount of sunlight provided to the plants

52. Which of the following household products is NOT correctly matched with the formula of the chemical it's associated with?

a. Salt, NaCl
b. Sugar, $C_{12}H_{22}O_{11}$
c. Hydrogen peroxide, H_2O_2
d. Chalk, $NaCO_3$

53. Which of the following is NOT a benefit of biodegradable plastic?

a. Biodegradable plastics reduce the volume of trash in landfills.
b. Biodegradable plastics help conserve petroleum supplies.
c. Biodegradable plastics are cheaper to produce than alternatives.
d. Biodegradable plastics lower the amount of energy used in production.

54. The Earth's magnetic field protects it from:

a. Excess heat from the Sun
b. Radio waves from black holes
c. Solar wind
d. Impacts from space debris

55. What is the speed of a wave with a frequency of 12 Hz and a wavelength of 3 meters?

a. 12 meters per second
b. 36 meters per second
c. 4 meters per second
d. 0.25 meters per second

56. A virus is actively replicating DNA in what stage?

a. Lysogenic cycle
b. Lytic cycle
c. Retrovirus
d. Provirus

57. Which of the following statements is NOT congruent with the theory of plate tectonics?

a. The continents were once connected in the large supercontinent Pangea.
b. The tectonic plates are part of the Earth's lithosphere.
c. Seafloor spreading is evidence of tectonic plate movement.
d. Subduction occurs at divergent boundaries.

58. When metamorphic rock is stressed unevenly during recrystallization, it can result in:

a. Foliation
b. Contact metamorphism
c. Regional metamorphism
d. Extrusion

59. What is the point of a phase diagram where a substance can exist as a solid, a liquid, and a gas?

a. Isothermal point
b. Isobaric point
c. Triple point
d. Critical point

60. Which of the following historical figures is NOT correctly matched with his contribution to modern science?

a. Louis Pasteur and the germ concept of disease
b. Thomas Edison and the theory of relativity
c. Johannes Kepler and the laws of planetary motion
d. Nicolaus Copernicus and the heliocentric view of the solar system

61. Which of the following is a vector quantity?

a. Distance
b. Speed
c. Velocity
d. Time

62. Students have just completed a lab. What can they do to be sure that their results are reliable?

a. Repeat the lab again
b. Compare their data to data collected in similar experiments
c. Measure all of their results twice with two different rulers
d. Make sure that their results confirm that their hypothesis was correct

63. The majority of the solar energy that reaches Earth is absorbed by:

a. Glaciers
b. Landmasses
c. Oceans
d. The Earth's atmosphere

64. Which of the following events immediately precedes a volcanic eruption?

a. A batholith forms beneath the Earth's surface.
b. Magma fills vertical and horizontal fractures in the Earth's crust, creating sills and dikes.
c. An oceanic plate is subducted by a continental plate.
d. A dike reaches the Earth's surface and a plume passes through it.

65. The most recently formed parts of the Earth's crust can be found at:

a. Subduction zones
b. Compressional boundaries
c. Extensional boundaries
d. Mid-ocean ridges

66. The pulley in the device below has no mass and is frictionless. The larger mass is 30 kg and the smaller mass is 20 kg. What is the acceleration of the masses?

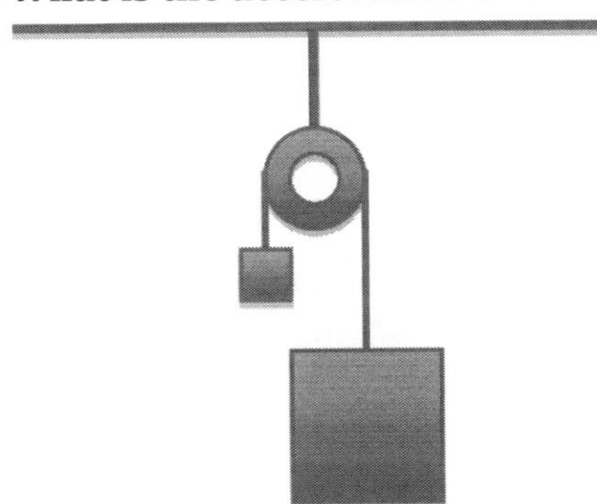

a. 0.5 m/s^2
b. 2.0 m/s^2
c. 9.8 m/s^2
d. 98 m/s^2

67. Which of the following is the mathematical principle used to calculate a user's position based on information from the GPS satellites in the user's area?

a. Triangulation
b. Trilateration
c. Quadlateration
d. Quadangulation

68. Which of the following is currently the greatest benefit of genetically modified crops?

a. Increased profits for farmers
b. Increased nutrition for consumers
c. Increased shelf life of foods
d. Decreased allergens for consumers

69. Which of the following factors directly contributes to soil erosion?

a. Air pollution from cars and factories
b. Use of pesticides
c. Deforestation and overgrazing
d. Water pollution caused by excess sedimentation

70. When using a microscope, which objective provides the greatest field of view?

a. 4X
b. 10X
c. 40X
d. 100X

71. Ammonia has a specific heat capacity greater than that of water. This means that:

a. Water vaporizes at a higher temperature than ammonia.
b. It takes more energy to increase the temperature of ammonia than it does to increase the temperature of water.
c. Water is always denser than ammonia.
d. Water is only denser than ammonia at higher temperatures.

72. Nuclear chain reactions, such as the kind that is exploited in nuclear power plants, are propagated by what subatomic particle(s)?

a. Protons
b. Neutrons
c. Electrons
d. Neutrons and protons

73. A bacterial mini-chromosome used in recombinant DNA technology is called a

a. Centromere
b. Telomere
c. Plasmid
d. Transposon

Refer to the following for question 74:

Diagram representing a cross section of a tree trunk

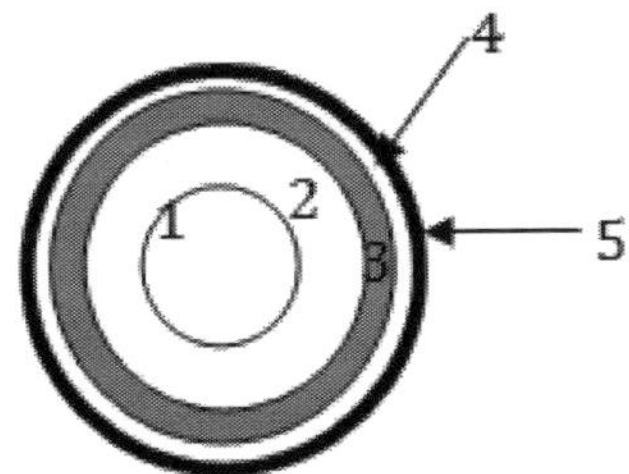

74. Which structure transports carbohydrates to the roots?

a. 1
b. 2
c. 3
d. 4

75. Suppose a moving railroad car collides with an identical stationary car and the two cars latch together. Ignoring friction, and assuming no deformation on impact, which of the following statements is true?

a. The speed of the first car decreases by half.
b. The collision is elastic.
c. The speed of the first car is doubled.
d. There is no determining the final speed because the collision was inelastic.

76. Which of the following is NOT a statement of one of the laws established by Isaac Newton?

a. The lateral pressure exerted by a moving fluid decreases as the fluid's speed increases.
b. For every action there is an opposite and equal reaction.
c. The acceleration of an object is directly related to the force applied to the object and inversely related to the object's mass.
d. The attraction between two objects is directly related to the masses of the objects and inversely related to the square of the distance between the two objects.

77. Which of the following structures is NOT present in gymnosperms?

a. Leaves
b. Pollen
c. Flowers
d. Stomata

78. Which of the following is NOT true about land reclamation?

a. Land for agricultural use may be reclaimed by draining submerged wetlands.
b. Land reclamation may destroy habitats and increase biodiversity.
c. Land reclamation creates new lands from ocean beds, riverbeds, or lakebeds.
d. Land reclamation may result in soil liquefaction during earthquakes.

79. Which has a greater moment of inertia about an axis through its center: a solid cylinder or a hollow cylinder? Both cylinders have the same mass and radius.

a. Solid cylinder
b. Hollow cylinder
c. Both have the same moment of inertia.
d. It depends on how quickly the cylinders are rolling.

80. A lead sphere 10 centimeters in diameter is attached to a 10-meter wire and suspended from a beam in a large warehouse. A lead sphere 1 meter in diameter is hung next to the smaller sphere, almost touching. Ignoring friction, which statement is true?

a. The small sphere will move slightly toward the big sphere, but the big sphere will not move.
b. The big sphere will move slightly toward the small sphere, but the small sphere will not move.
c. Neither sphere will move.
d. Both spheres will move slightly toward each other.

Answer Key and Explanations for Test #1

1. D: Water in the liquid state generally has a higher density than water in the solid state (ice). Unlike most other substances, which become progressively denser as they grow colder, water's density only increases until it reaches a maximum density around 4 °C, after which it begins to decrease as the temperature drops further.

2. C: Weighing the benefits to people and the economy against the risks is why governments would conduct a risk-benefit analysis before making decisions about city planning and development. Answer A, which states that governments must know what the benefits of a new development are for people and the economy in order to persuade opponents and the public who are against it, would be incorrect because the intention would be to build regardless of risk. Answer D, which suggests that the benefits to people and the economy can be used to ignore the risks associated with any new development, would also be incorrect as it would be unethical to ignore the risks.

3. D: A hypothesis predicts what the experimenter thinks is going to happen and why. It is based on prior knowledge and research. An experiment is designed to test the hypothesis. Without a hypothesis, an experiment cannot be designed or performed.

4. A: The amplitude of waves that cross/interfere is the sum of the instantaneous height at the point the two waves cross. In this case, one wave is at its peak amplitude A: The other wave, in a trough, is at its minimum amplitude $-A$. Since these waves are at opposite heights, their sum is $A + -A = 0$. Had the waves both been peaking, the sum would be $A + A = 2A$. If they had both been at a minimum, the sum would be $-2A$.

5. C: Proteins are large polypeptides, composed of many amino acids linked together by an amide bond. DNA and RNA are nucleic acids made up of repeating nucleotides. Carbohydrates are long chains of sugars. Triglycerides are fats and are composed of a glycerol molecule and three fatty acids.

6. A: Nuclear reactions convert mass into energy ($\mathrm{E} = \mathrm{mc}^2$). The mass of products is always less than that of the starting materials since some mass is now energy.

7. C: Deforestation causes the loss of numerous trees. Trees contain carbon dioxide (CO_2), the leading contributor to climate change. The process of deforestation releases some of this CO_2 into the atmosphere, especially if the wood is burned. CO_2 is also discharged from the machinery that is used in the process of deforestation. Deforestation contributes to an estimated ten percent of all greenhouse emissions. Trees also remove carbon dioxide from the atmosphere through a process called sequestering. Less trees mean less carbon dioxide is sequestered resulting in an increase of the carbon dioxide in the atmosphere.

8. C: Advantages of biomass energy include that it's renewable, carbon neutral, and abundant. A disadvantage of biomass energy include that it requires space and may be inefficient.

9. C: Chemicals should not be stored routinely on bench tops. Each chemical should be stored in a location for that specific type of chemical. When in use, chemicals may be temporarily kept on bench tops, but only in the quantities that are required for that particular situation. Chemicals should be returned to an appropriate location after use.

10. C: The pH probes should be stored according to the manufacturer's instructions. In general, pH probes should never be stored in water or stored dry without first draining the electrode. They should always be stored in an appropriate buffer or reference electrolyte, which is usually a 3M – 4M potassium chloride solution.

11. B: Dalton stated that atoms are hard spheres. Thomson proposed the plum pudding model, in which electrons are embedded in a sphere of positive charge. Rutherford introduced the planetary model, in which electrons circularly orbit a small central nucleus. Bohr's model stated that electrons move in regions of space called orbits. This would later be expanded to "orbitals" of the later quantum-mechanical model.

12. D: In the lysogenic cycle, viral DNA gets incorporated into the DNA of the host. A virus in this dormant stage is called a provirus. Eventually, an external cue may trigger the virus to excise itself and begin the lytic cycle.

13. B: It is true that the asthenosphere is hotter and more fluid than the lithosphere. The asthenosphere, also called the upper mantle, is the hot, fluid layer of the Earth's mantle upon which the lithosphere, or crust, is situated. Heat is transferred within the asthenosphere through a process called convection, which sometimes causes movement in the tectonic plates that make up the lithosphere.

14. C: All three laws of motion are operating, but the third law (forces come in equal and opposite pairs) best explains the motion. The first law (inertia) is shown from the fact that the balloon doesn't move until a force acts upon it. The second law (F = ma) is shown because you can see the force and the acceleration. The force comes from the contraction of the rubber balloon. The stretched rubber exerts a force on the air inside the balloon. This causes the air to accelerate in accordance with the second law. You can't see this acceleration because the air is invisible and because it is all the air in the room that the balloon is exerting a force on. However, the air in the room exerts an equal and opposite force on the balloon (this is Newton's third law), which causes the balloon to accelerate in the direction it did.

15. D: When diluting acids, the acid should always be added to the water. This way, if splashing occurs, only water is splashed out of the beaker. Additionally, this procedure ensures that only a small amount of acid is present in a much larger volume of water. This is especially important when diluting sulfuric acid, because large amounts of heat may be released in the hydration process, which could cause a small amount of water to boil rapidly.

16. B: Phosphorus is in the third period, so the outermost levels must be $3s$, $3p$. Phosphorus is in Group 5A, which indicates that it has 5 valence electrons. To fill the $3s$ and $3p$, 2 electrons first fill the s orbital, and then the remaining 3 electrons enter the p orbitals, making $3s^2 3p^3$.

17. D: Strip mining of coal destroys landscapes, forest, and wildlife habitats. Strip mining also causes dust and noise pollution and may contaminate groundwater. Underground coal mining lowers the water table and changes the flow of groundwater and streams.

18. D: Since this is a head-on elastic collision, you could use conservation of kinetic energy and momentum to actually solve this problem. However, in this case, you only need to think through the answers to arrive at a correct conclusion. After the ball is struck, it won't be going 0 m/s. And since this is an elastic collision, and it is hit by a much larger ball, it must be going faster than the larger ball was originally moving. Therefore, the ball will be moving at more than 10 m/s. If this were an inelastic collision where the balls stuck together, the balls' final velocity would be less than 10 m/s.

19. C: To convert from degrees Celsius to Kelvin, add 273. 75 °C is equivalent to 348 K. Both X and Y have lower boiling points, which means that they will each boil in the water bath. Z will never become warm enough to boil.

20. D: There are only 2 significant digits in A. Answers B and C have 5 significant digits. Answer D has 6 significant digits. Trailing zeroes after a decimal point are considered significant because it implies a certain level of specificity. Trailing numbers in a whole number that does not contain a decimal are not significant.

21. C: The question asks how much friction is needed to start the block moving, which means you need to calculate the force of static friction. If the question had asked about the force needed to keep the object moving at a constant speed, you would calculate the force of kinetic friction. Here, the force of static friction is equal to $\mu_{\text{static}} \times N$, where N is the Normal force. The normal force (N) on the plastic block is the weight of the block ($w = mg$) which is $10 \text{ kg} \times 9.8 \text{ m/s}^2 = 98$ newtons. The force of static friction is $0.6 \times 98 \text{ N} = 59 \text{ N}$. Answer B is the force of kinetic friction, once the block starts moving. (Note: molecular bonding and abrasion cause friction. When the surfaces are in motion, the bonding is less strong, so the coefficient of kinetic friction is less than the coefficient of static friction. Therefore, more force is required to start the box moving than to keep it moving.)

22. D: Isaac Newton proposed the particle or corpuscular theory of light. Huygens proposed the wave theory of light. Maxwell showed that light can be modeled as an electromagnetic wave. Einstein described electromagnetic radiation as bundles of energy proportional to frequency in the quantum theory of light.

23. C: This is a problem of free fall in two dimensions. A thrown ball without air resistance will only be subjected to one force, gravity. This causes a downward acceleration of exactly 9.8 m/s^2 on all objects, regardless of their size, speed or position. Note: since the ball was thrown directly upwards, the horizontal acceleration is 0 m/s^2 and the horizontal speed at all times is 0 m/s. B is wrong because the force of gravity is always pointed downward and never changes direction.

24. B: A variable is something that is changed in the experiment. It is being tested against other similar things. In this experiment, the variable is the type of window cleaner.

25. D: In 1912, Alfred Wegener proposed that the continents once formed a single land mass called Pangaea, but have since drifted apart. Theories about the Earth's magnetic fields and plate tectonics did not emerge until years later. Once they did, they helped produce evidence to support Wegener's theory.

26. D: Isotopes of the same element must have the same chemical behavior, and (A), (B), and (C) all represent, in one form or another, chemical behavior. Isotopes differ in mass, and this can be used to separate them by some appropriate physical property.

27. C: Alternation of generations means the alternation between the diploid and haploid phases in plants.

28. D: Conjugation is direct transfer of plasmid DNA between bacteria through a pilus. The F plasmid contains genes that enable bacteria to produce pili and is often the DNA that is transferred between bacteria.

29. B: A year is determined by the number of days it takes for a body to make one revolution around the Sun. So a Martian year would be the number of days it takes for Mars to orbit the Sun.

30. D: When adding, the answer should be rounded to the same number of decimal places as the measurement with the fewest decimal places. The total mass is obtained by adding up all four measurements. This yields 35.5918. Since the first and second masses are precise to only a hundredth of a gram, your answer can't be more precise than this. The number 35.5918, when rounded to two decimal places, is 35.59.

31. B: Glass cleaner traditionally was a 5% ammonia solution. Recently most glass cleaners are more environmentally friendly solutions containing much less ammonia. Bleach is a solution of 3-6% sodium hypochlorite.

32. A: In a closed system (when you ignore outside interactions), the total momentum is constant and conserved. The total energy would also be conserved, although not the sum of the potential and kinetic energy. Some of the energy from the collision would be turned into thermal energy (heat) for example. Nor is the total velocity conserved, even though the velocity is a component of the momentum, since the momentum also depends on the mass of the cars. The impulse is a force over time that causes the momentum of a body to change. It doesn't make sense to think of impulse as conserved, since it's not necessarily constant throughout a collision.

33. B: In ferns, the mature diploid plant is called a sporophyte. Sporophytes undergo meiosis to produce spores, which develop into gametophytes, which produce gametes.

34. A: Transcription is the process of creating an RNA strand from a DNA template. All forms of RNA—for example, mRNA, tRNA, and rRNA—are products of transcription.

35. A: If diluted, acetic acid may be disposed of by sink or sewer. Vinegar is a 5% acetic acid solution and is commonly used in the kitchen. In general, alkanoic acids with 5 or fewer carbon atoms, such as acetic acid, butyric acid, and formic acid, may be disposed of by sink or sewer. Chemicals such as benzene, acetone, and mercury should never be disposed of by sink or sewer.

36. C: The data is relatively consistent with the exception of trial 1. When an experiment is repeated using the same process multiple times, the data from each trial should be very similar or the same. The results of trial 1 indicate that an error may have occurred in the procedure yielding inaccurate results.

37. B: The trend within any column of the periodic table is that electronegativity decreases going down the column.

38. A: Repetition is the only way to prove that an experiment is reliable. If an experiment can't be successfully repeated with the same outcome, one cannot determine that the experimental results are valid. Repetition is the key to scientific progress.

39. D: Stomata are openings on leaves that allow for gas exchange, which is essential for photosynthesis. Stomata are surrounded by guard cells, which open and close based on their turgidity.

40. B: The newton can be defined in terms of the fundamental units of meters, kilograms, and seconds as $\text{N} = \text{kg} \times \text{m/s}^2$, so it is not a fundamental unit. Statement II is a result of $F = ma$, Newton's second law, which is true. If $F = 0$ N, then the acceleration is $0\ \text{m/s}^2$. If the acceleration is $0\ \text{m/s}^2$, then the speed is $0\ \text{m/s}$ or a nonzero constant. This is a nonverbal statement of Newton's first law, meaning Newton's first law can be derived from his second law. Newton's second law cannot be derived from the universal law of gravity.

41. C: Displacement is a vector that indicates the change in the location of an object. Answer A would be correct if the question asked for the total distance the person walked or if the person didn't change direction. If the person turned around 180°, the displacement could be as small as 5 meters. If the person changed directions only a fraction of a degree, the displacement's magnitude would be *less* than 13 meters, not as *large* as 13 meters.

42. D: The table states that a person's mass remains the same, but weight will fluctuate with the force of gravity. It also states that the more gravity acting on an object, the more the object will weigh. Neptune has a greater gravitational force than Earth, so the person's weight would increase.

43. C: John Dalton proposed the atomic theory of matter in 1803. He stated that each element consists of tiny, indivisible particles called atoms. He did not believe that an atom could be further broken down.

44. D: Mendeleev was able to connect the trends of the different elements' behaviors and develop a table that showed the periodicity of the elements and their relationship to each other.

45. C: Physical weathering of rocks can be caused by changes in temperature and pressure, as well as the freezing and thawing of water on the surfaces of rocks. Oxidation is a chemical process, not a physical one. Therefore, it is considered an example of chemical rather than physical weathering.

46. A: The lithification process results in the formation of sedimentary rocks. During lithification, existing rock is compacted and liquid is squeezed from its pores. Eventually, the rock is cemented together, resulting in sedimentary rock.

47. B: The answer can be determined because the rate of acceleration is uniform. Since the acceleration is 5 m/s^2, the velocity increases by 5 m/s every second. If it starts at 20 m/s, after 1 second it will be going 25 m/s. After another second it will be going 30 m/s, so the total time is 2 seconds. You can also calculate this time by using the average speed. Since the object undergoes uniform acceleration, the average speed is 25 m/s. Using the distance traveled, the same result is obtained. $t = \frac{d}{v} = \frac{50 \text{ meters}}{25 \text{ m/s}} = 2$ seconds.

48. D: Resonance structures have the same atoms connected to the same atoms, but differ only in electronic structure amongst the atoms. Isomers are molecules that have the same formula but differ in structure. Structural isomers differ in how the atoms are bonded to each other. Stereoisomers are isomers that have the same bonding structure but different arrangements, for example, cis- and trans- isomers.

49. C: Minerals that form on the sea floor from discarded shells are most likely part of the carbonate class. Minerals that form in karst regions and evaporitic settings may also be carbonates. Examples of minerals in the carbonate class include aragonite, dolomite, calcite, and siderite.

50. B: Plutonic, or intrusive, rock forms deep beneath the Earth's surface and cools slowly. Volcanic, or extrusive, rock solidifies at or near the surface. Hypabyssal rock forms below the Earth's surface, but not at a depth as great as plutonic rock. Detrital rock is a type of sedimentary rock.

51. B: A control is a variable in the experiment that has not been changed by the experimenter but is subjected to the same processes as the other tested components. Plants are usually provided only water; these are being tested against bleach, salt, and diet soda, all of which are not regularly used to water a plant. The control acts as a reference point for comparison of the results,

52. D: Chalk is a form of calcium carbonate, which has the molecular formula $CaCO_3$.

53. C: While biodegradable plastics are renewable, it is still more expensive to produce them for now.

54. C: The Earth's magnetic field protects it from solar wind. Solar wind is a stream of highly charged radioactive particles that emanate from the Sun, and these particles are deflected by the magnetic field. The magnetic field is shaped like a bowl that covers the side of the Earth facing the Sun. It deflects most solar particles, but some are trapped in the Van Allen belt. Particularly strong bursts of solar wind allow particles to pass through this belt into the Earth's ionosphere and upper atmosphere, creating geomagnetic storms and auroras.

55. B: The speed of a wave is the product of its wavelength and frequency. $V = \lambda f$. Here, $V = 3 \times 12 = 36 \text{ m/s}$.

56. B: In the lytic cycle, viruses use host resources to produce viral DNA and proteins in order to create new viruses. In the process, they destroy the host cell by lysing it. For this reason, actively replicating viruses are said to be in the lytic cycle.

57. D: Subduction occurs at convergent boundaries. Subduction is the process that occurs when two tectonic plates collide and one plate moves under the other plate.

58. A: When metamorphic rock is stressed unevenly during recrystallization, it can result in foliation. Foliation is characterized by banded rock, and it occurs when certain types of minerals are reoriented during recrystallization due to uneven shortening or compression of the rock.

59. C: A triple point on a phase diagram indicates a precise temperature and pressure where a substance can simultaneously exist as a solid, a liquid, and a gas. Isothermal means constant temperature and would refer to a vertical line rather than a point. Isobaric means constant pressure and would refer to a horizontal line rather than a point. The critical point indicates a particular temperature and pressure beyond which the substance is neither a liquid nor a gas, but a supercritical fluid.

60. B: Albert Einstein is known for both the special theory of relativity and the general theory of relativity. Thomas Edison was an inventor best known for inventing the light bulb and phonograph.

61. C: Vectors have a magnitude (e.g., 5 meters/second) and direction (e.g., towards north). Of the choices listed, only velocity is defined as a vector. Speed, distance, and time are all quantities that have a size but not a direction. That's why, for example, a car's speedometer reads 35 miles/hour, but does not indicate your direction of travel.

62. A: To be the more precise, the students could complete the lab again. In fact, all scientific laws have been developed by being tested over and over again through repetitive scientific experiment.

63. C: The majority of the solar energy that reaches Earth is absorbed by the oceans, which make up 71 percent of the Earth's surface. Because of water's high specific heat capacity, oceans can absorb and store large quantities of heat, thus preventing drastic increases in the overall atmospheric temperature.

64. D: A volcano occurs when a dike (a vertical fracture in the Earth's crust that fills with magma) reaches the Earth's surface and a plume (a spurt of magma) passes through it. Batholiths are large masses of igneous rock that form beneath the Earth's surface, and a sill is a horizontal fracture in the Earth's crust that fills with magma. When an oceanic plate is subducted by a continental plate, it results in the formation of mountain ranges.

65. D: The most recently formed parts of the Earth's crust can be found at mid-ocean ridges. New crust forms here when magma erupts from these ridges and pushes preexisting crust horizontally towards the continental plates. Such ridges include the Mid-Atlantic Ridge and the East Pacific Rise.

66. B: The weight of the masses is determined from $W = mg$. In this case, there is a force to the left/down of 20 kg × 9.8 m/s^2 = 196 N, and a force to the right/down of 30 kg × 9.8 m/s^2 = 294 N. The net force is 98 N to the right/down. This force is moving both masses, however, which have a total mass of 50 kg. Using $F = ma$ and solving for acceleration gives $a = \frac{98 \text{ N}}{50 \text{ kg}} = 2 \text{ m/s}^2$.

67. B: A communication GPS receiver uses trilateration by timing signals from at least four satellites in the Global Positioning System. This allows it to determine its 3D position (latitude, longitude, and altitude) while also correcting for the receiver's clock error. Trilateration determines position, speed, and elevation. Trilateration differs from triangulation in that trilateration calculations use distances, while triangulation calculations use angles.

68. A: Currently, the greatest benefit of genetically modified crops is to the farmer, with herbicide-resistant and pest-resistant crops. This increases profits and makes farming a little easier. Currently, foods made from genetically modified crops do not show significant increases in nutrition or shelf life. One of the greatest concerns regarding foods produced from genetically modified crops is the possibility of introducing new allergens into the food supply.

69. C: Overgrazing and deforestation directly contribute to soil erosion by destroying the natural ground cover that normally prevents soil from being washed and blown away. These activities can ultimately result in desertification, which renders land unsuitable for agriculture.

70. A: The field of view is the diameter of the circle of light that is seen when one looks into the microscope. As the power of the objective increases, the field of view gets smaller. Therefore, the objective with the greatest field of view is the one with the lowest power.

71. B: The fact that water's specific heat capacity is second only to that of ammonia means that it takes more energy to increase the temperature of ammonia than it does to increase the temperature of water. Specific heat capacity refers to the amount of energy required to increase the temperature of a substance by one degree Celsius. Ammonia has the highest specific heat capacity of all substances, and the specific heat capacity of water is the second highest.

72. B: Neutrons are neutral in charge, and can impact a nucleus in order to break it.

73. C: Plasmids are small circular pieces of DNA found in bacteria. Plasmids are widely used in recombinant DNA technology. They are cut with restriction enzymes and DNA of interest is ligated to them. They can then easily be used to transform bacteria.

74. D: The phloem is the pipeline through which carbohydrates are transported to the roots. It is located outside of the xylem and lives for only a short time before becoming part of the outer bark.

75. A: A collision is considered elastic when neither object loses any kinetic energy. Since the cars latch together, this can't be the case. You could prove this by calculating the cars' kinetic energy: $KE = \frac{1}{2}mv^2$. If the railroad cars had bumpers instead of couplers, the moving car would stop and transfer all its momentum and kinetic energy to the stationary car, causing an elastic collision. In a closed system like this one, however, the conservation of momentum is an absolute law, where an object's momentum is its mass times its velocity. There are no external forces acting on the two cars. The only forces are between the two cars themselves. The momentum before the collision is the same as the momentum after the collision: $mv_{initial} + m\left(0\frac{\text{m}}{\text{s}}\right) = mv_{final} + mv_{final}$. So $mv_{initial} = 2mv_{final}$, and $v_{initial} = 2v_{final}$. Thus, the final velocity is half the initial velocity.

76. A: Bernoulli's principle states that the lateral pressure exerted by a moving fluid decreases as the fluid's speed increases. This principle is named after Daniel Bernoulli.

77. C: Gymnosperms reproduce by producing pollen and ovules, but they do not have flowers. Instead, their reproductive structures are cones or cone-like structures.

78. B: While land reclamation destroys nearby habitats, it doesn't increase biodiversity. The destruction of habitats leads to a decrease in biodiversity.

79. B: The moment of inertia of a point mass, m, about any axis is given by mR^2, where R is the distance from the axis. The moment of inertia of a solid object is calculated by imagining that the object is made up of point masses and adding the moments of inertia of the point masses. The average radius of the particles in a hollow cylinder will be R (all the mass is at radius R). For a solid cylinder, however, the average radius is less than R, meaning the overall moment of inertia will be smaller. The moment of inertia of a cylinder of thickness $R_2 - R_1$, where R_1 and R_2 are the inner and outer radii, respectively, is calculated by $\frac{1}{2}m({R_1}^2 + {R_2}^2)$. For a solid cylinder, $R_1 = 0$ meters. For a hollow cylinder, $R_1 = R_2$.

80. D: There will be a gravitational force of attraction between the two spheres determined by the universal constant of gravity, the distance between the spheres, and the mass of the spheres. Since both objects are affected by this force (remember, Newton's third law says the force needs to be equal and opposite), both objects will experience a slight acceleration and start moving towards each other a tiny amount (when we ignore friction). Using $\text{F} = \text{ma}$, you know that the less massive sphere will experience a larger acceleration than the more massive one.

Practice Test #2

1. Which of the following devices changes chemical energy into electrical energy?

a. battery
b. closed electric circuit
c. generator
d. transformer

2. Darwin's idea that evolution occurs by the gradual accumulation of small changes can be described as:

a. Punctuated equilibrium
b. Phyletic gradualism
c. Convergent evolution
d. Adaptive radiation

3. Genetic engineering:

a. Is a form of human reproduction
b. Always involves using restriction enzymes to cut DNA
c. Always involves transient expression of genes
d. Often involves using nucleases to cut DNA

4. A student is measuring morning and afternoon temperatures for a school project using a thermal infrared gun instrument. The instrument is calibrated incorrectly and produces a cold bias of $\frac{7}{10}$ of a degree in all the temperature measurements. How should the student deal with this error?

a. The student should recalibrate the instrument and redo the project.
b. Since it is not a major error, the student can ignore it.
c. This is a systematic error and the student should take it into consideration when analyzing the results by increasing the temperatures $\frac{7}{10}$ of a degree.
d. This is a random error so the student should only mention it as a potential problem in interpreting the results.

5. Which of the following conditions and chemical pairs is an example of a buffer?

a. Homeostasis; H_2CO_3/HCO_3^-
b. Water has a neutral pH; $(H_3O)^+/OH^-$
c. Copper can be electroplated onto tin; Cu^+/Sn^{2+}
d. Aluminum hydroxide is not soluble; Al^{3+}/OH^-

6. A population of pea plants has 25% dwarf plants and 75% tall plants. The tall allele, *T* is dominant to the dwarf allele, *t*. What is the frequency of the *T* allele?

a. 0.75
b. 0.67
c. 0.5
d. 0.25

7. What will happen to light waves as they hit a convex lens?

a. They will be refracted and converge.
b. They will be refracted and diverge.
c. They will be reflected and converge.
d. They will be reflected and diverge.

8. After a science laboratory exercise, some solutions remain unused and are left over. What should be done with these solutions?

a. Dispose of the solutions according to local disposal procedures.
b. Empty the solutions into the sink and rinse with warm water and soap.
c. Ensure the solutions are secured in closed containers and throw away.
d. Store the solutions in a secured, dry place for later use.

9. Which of the following does NOT obey the law of independent assortment?

a. Two genes on opposite ends of a chromosome
b. Flower color and height in snapdragons
c. Two genes on separate chromosomes
d. Two genes next to each other on a chromosome

10. Which of the following ecosystems is most likely to have an inverted biomass pyramid?

a. Forest ecosystem
b. Tundra ecosystem
c. Desert ecosystem
d. Aquatic ecosystem

11. Which of the following statements about a solid metal sphere with a net charge is true?

a. If the charge is positive, it will be distributed uniformly throughout the sphere.
b. The charge will be distributed uniformly at the surface of the sphere.
c. The charge will leave the sphere.
d. The electric field will be tangent to the surface of the sphere.

12. Which of the following organisms is likely to have the greatest quantity of mercury in its body?

a. Mosquitoes
b. Frogs
c. Filter-feeding fish
d. Fish-eating birds

13. Which of the following life forms appeared first on Earth?

a. Eukaryotes
b. Arthropods
c. Prokaryotes
d. Amphibians

14. The frequency of ocean waves is measured by:

a. The vertical distance between a wave's crest and trough
b. The horizontal distance between the crests of two subsequent waves
c. The time between two subsequent wave crests
d. The number of wave crests that pass a given point each second

15. Which of the following equations for sound waves correctly relates frequency to wavelength and speed of sound?

a. $f \times \lambda = v$
b. $f = \lambda \times v$
c. $f = \lambda + v$
d. $f \times \lambda \times v = 1$

16. During primary succession, which species would most likely be a pioneer species?

a. Lichens
b. Fir trees
c. Mosquitoes
d. Dragonflies

17. Chemical compounds are formed when:

a. Valence electrons from atoms of two different elements are shared or transferred.
b. Valence electrons from multiple atoms of a single element are shared or transferred.
c. The nuclei of two atoms are joined together.
d. The nucleus of an atom is split.

18. Redshift is observed when:

a. A light-emitting object moves away from an observer.
b. A star begins to decrease the amount of light it emits.
c. A light-emitting object moves toward an observer.
d. A magnetic field bends observed light.

19. Which graph segments below represent constant speed?

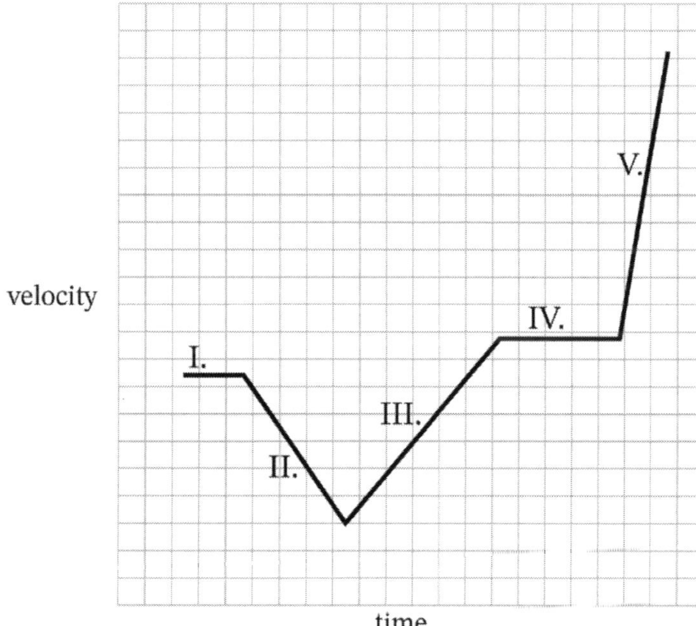

a. I and IV
b. III and V
c. II, III, and V
d. II and III

20. Which graph segment below represents the greatest acceleration?

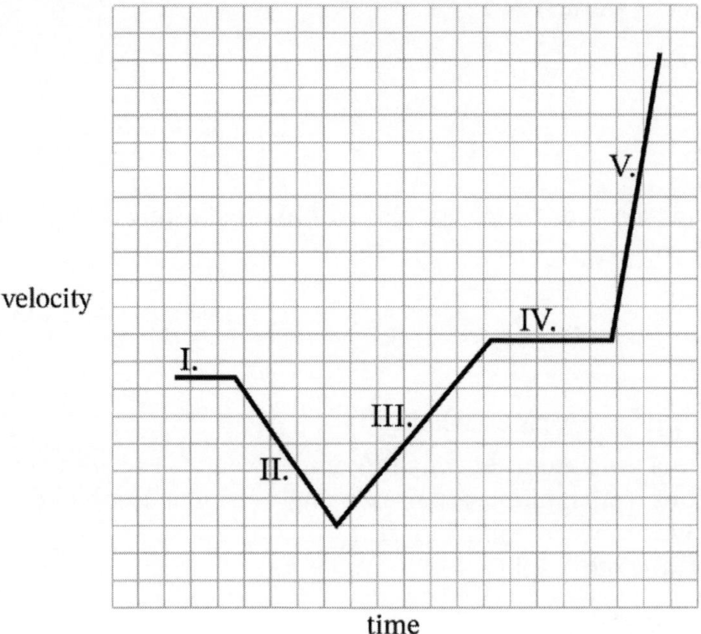

a. II
b. III
c. V
d. III and V

21. Which of the following is a trait that results from disruptive selection?

a. Insecticide resistance
b. Only male peacocks having colorful plumage
c. Some birds having significantly large bills than others within the same species
d. Human height

22. Broadly speaking, learning can be divided into what two categories?

a. active and passive
b. theoretical and practical
c. hands-on and minds-on
d. inquiry-based and book-based

23. The electrolysis of water is an example of which of the following?

a. An adiabatic process
b. A chemical change
c. A synthesis reaction
d. Reverse osmosis

24. Which of the following creates an electromagnet?

a. Rapidly spinning and rotating electrons inside an iron bar
b. An iron bar moving inside a coil of wire that contains a current
c. The movement of electrons through a complete circuit
d. Convection currents within the liquid core of Earth's interior

25. Which of the following habitats would provide an opportunity for secondary succession?

a. A retreating glacier
b. Burned cropland
c. A newly formed volcanic island
d. A 500-year-old forest

Refer to the following for question 26:

A biome featuring scrubby plants and small evergreen trees has a hot, dry summer followed by a wetter winter. The following food chain exists in the biome:

$$tree \rightarrow caterpillar \rightarrow frog \rightarrow snake \rightarrow hawk \rightarrow vulture \rightarrow worm$$

26. What role do vultures play in the food chain?

a. Scavengers
b. Detritivores
c. Primary carnivores
d. Herbivores

27. A ball is thrown and the distance it traveled is measured. Which data set corresponds to the graph below?

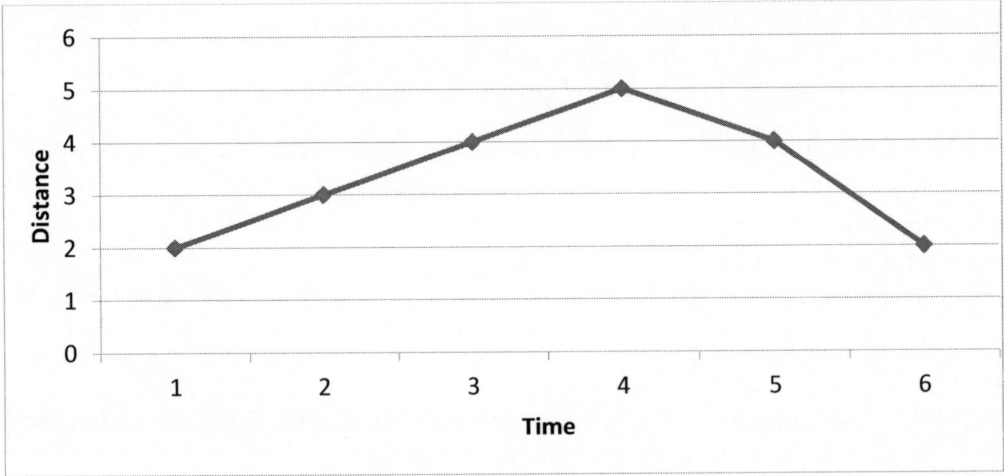

a.

Time	Distance
1	2
2	4
3	6
4	8
5	9

b.

Time	Distance
1	2
3	4
5	6
7	8
9	9

c.

Time	Distance
2	0
4	1
6	3
8	5
9	7

d.

Time	Distance
1	2
2	3
3	4
4	5
5	4
6	2

28. A motorcycle weighs twice as much as a bicycle and is moving twice as fast. Which of the following statements is true?

a. The motorcycle has four times as much kinetic energy as the bicycle.
b. The motorcycle has eight times as much kinetic energy as the bicycle.
c. The bicycle and the motorcycle have the same kinetic energy.
d. The bicycle has four times as much kinetic energy as the motorcycle.

Refer to the following for questions 29–30:

> *A student is conducting an experiment using a ball that is attached to the end of a string, forming a pendulum. The student pulls the ball back so that it is at an angle to its resting position. As the student releases the ball, it swings forward and backward. The student measures the time it takes the ball to make one complete period. A period is defined as the time it takes the ball to swing forward and back again to its starting position. This is repeated using different string lengths.*

29. What would be an appropriate control variable for this experiment?

a. The period
b. The length of the string
c. The mass of the ball
d. The color of the ball

30. The student formed the following hypothesis:

> *Lengthening the string of the pendulum will increase the time it takes the ball to make one complete period.*

What correction would you have the student make to the hypothesis to make it follow the classical hypothesis model?

a. Turn it into an "if/then" statement.
b. Change "will increase" to "increases."
c. Switch the order of the sentence so that the phrase about the period comes first, and the phrase about the string's length is last.
d. No corrections are needed.

31. What is the scientific definition of work?

a. The amount of energy used to accomplish a job
b. The force used to move a mass over a distance
c. The amount of energy used per unit of time
d. Energy stored in an object due to its position

32. Which of the following diseases has been eradicated by immunization?

a. Polio
b. Mumps
c. Measles
d. Smallpox

33. When heat is removed from water during condensation, which of the following are formed.

a. Atoms
b. Covalent bonds
c. Intermolecular bonds
d. Ionic bonds

Refer to the following for question 34:

A chemistry experiment is performed to determine the effect of a nonvolatile solute on the boiling point of water. Three trials are performed in which 10 mg, 20 mg, and 30 mg of salt are added to 500 mL of distilled water. Each solution is heated on a hot plate, and the elevated boiling points are recorded.

34. What is the purpose of conducting this experiment?

a. To test a hypothesis
b. To collect data
c. To identify a control state
d. To choose variables

35. Several people were asked to jump on a large trampoline, one at a time, to see who could jump the highest. The results were recorded in the data table below.

Person	Weight	Highest Jump
Sarah	59 kg	1.35 m
Mark	75 kg	1.81 m
Isaac	78 kg	1.93 m
Valerie	64 kg	1.47 m
Crystal	66 kg	1.57 m

Based on the data, what can be concluded about the relationship between weight and jumping height?

a. The more a person weighs, the higher he or she could jump
b. The less a person weighs, the higher he or she could jump
c. A person's weight does not affect how high he or she was able to jump
d. The taller the person is, the higher he or she could jump

36. A calorimeter is used to measure changes in:

a. Heat
b. Mass
c. Weight
d. Volume

37. In the field of stratigraphy, the relative ages of rocks may be determined by examining which of the following types of evidence?

a. The dates the rocks were formed and the ages of fossils deposited within the rocks
b. Evidence of changes in detrital remanent magnetism when the rock was deposited
c. The vertical layering pattern of the rock
d. All of the above

38. Which statement correctly describes the elastic limit of a metal rod?

a. The elastic limit occurs when a deformed object will no longer return to its original shape.
b. The elastic limit occurs when the rod breaks.
c. The elastic limit occurs when the stress stops producing a strain.
d. The elastic limit assumes that the forces between molecules in a metal act like springs.

39. Which of the following statements about galaxies is true?

a. Galaxies are the only structures in the universe that do not contain dark matter.
b. Galaxies are gravitationally bound, meaning structures within the galaxy orbit around its center.
c. Galaxies typically contain over one trillion stars.
d. Galaxies are composed of clusters and superclusters.

40. In the field of geology, the term "uniformitarianism" refers to the belief that:

a. Catastrophic events like mass extinctions are the main forces that have shaped the Earth.
b. The Earth's crust has not undergone any dramatic changes since its formation.
c. The natural forces that shape the Earth have remained relatively constant over geologic time.
d. The Earth's stratigraphy is more or less uniform at any given geographic location.

41. In the diagram shown below, four wheels are in contact such that each wheel turns the opposite direction from the wheels it is touching. Wheel A is being turned clockwise by a force as shown. Which statement about wheel D is correct?

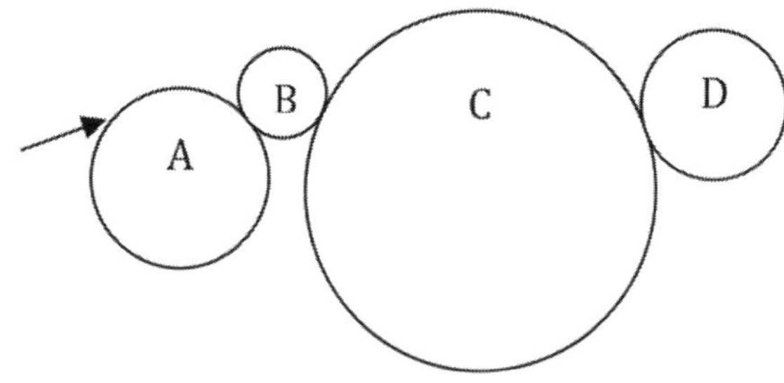

a. Wheel D does not turn at all because there are too many wheels between it and wheel A
b. Wheel D does not turn at all because it is not touching wheel C
c. Wheel D turns counterclockwise
d. Wheel D turns clockwise

42. Which element will most likely form a covalently bonded compound when it bonds with sulfur?

a. Argon (Ar)
b. Iron (Fe)
c. Lithium (Li)
d. Oxygen (O)

43. Which set of scientific thinkers is related to the study of chemistry?

a. Newton, Einstein, Feynman, and Hawking
b. Hooke, Pasteur, Watson & Crick, and Jacob & Monod
c. Ibn Hayyan, Lavoisier, Mendeleev, and Curie
d. Hutton, Darwin, Cuvier, and Wegener

44. The Coriolis effect in the Earth's oceans is caused by:

a. The Earth's rotation
b. The Earth's magnetic field
c. Variations in the density of seawater
d. The Gulf Stream

45. A circuit consists of a battery and a resistor. An ammeter is used to measure the current in the circuit and is connected in series to the circuit. Which of the following is true?

a. The current flowing in the resistor increases.
b. The current flowing in the resistor decreases.
c. The voltage drop across the resistor increases.
d. The current flowing in the resistor remains the same.

46. Which of the following statements correctly describes a difference between surface and subsurface ocean currents?

a. Subsurface currents are caused only by temperature variations, while surface currents are caused by changes in air pressure.
b. Subsurface currents are caused by temperature and density variations, while surface currents are caused by changes in air pressure.
c. Subsurface currents are caused by temperature and density variations, while surface currents are caused by wind.
d. Surface currents are caused by changes in air temperature, while subsurface currents are caused by changes in water temperature.

47. When using a light microscope, how is the total magnification determined?

a. By multiplying the ocular lens power by the objective being used
b. By looking at the objective you are using only
c. By looking at the ocular lens power only
d. By multiplying the objective you are using by two

48. When the accumulation of snow and ice exceeds ablation, which of the following occurs as a direct result?

a. An iceberg breaks free from a glacier.
b. A glacier gradually forms.
c. A glacier slowly erodes.
d. A lake forms within a glacier.

49. When light from a single source strikes two slits, alternating bright and dark lines appear on a screen on the far side. What is the best explanation for this phenomenon?

a. Doppler shift
b. Diffraction and interference
c. Chromatic aberration
d. Total internal reflection

50. Which of the following is the major way in which carbon is released into the environment?

a. Transpiration
b. Respiration
c. Fixation
d. Sedimentation

51. When a population reaches its carrying capacity:

a. Other populations will be forced out of the habitat.
b. Density-dependent factors no longer play a role.
c. Density-independent factors no longer play a role.
d. The population growth rate approaches zero.

52. The Cosmological Principle is best described as:

a. An assumption that cannot be tested empirically because it has no observable implications
b. A scientific hypothesis that has been repeatedly validated in empirical tests
c. A working assumption that has testable structural consequences
d. A law of physics that defies empirical testing

53. The state of matter in which atoms have the strongest bond is:

a. Plasma
b. Liquid
c. Solid
d. Gas

54. A nucleus absorbs a neutron and undergoes a fission reaction. Which of the following statements explains why this happens?

a. The nucleus is more stable with the additional neutron.
b. The new nucleus is unstable.
c. Energy is released.
d. The binding energy per nucleon decreases.

55. Which of the following of Lamarck's evolutionary ideas turned out to be true?

a. Natural selection
b. Organisms naturally transform into increasingly complex organisms
c. Inheritance of acquired characters
d. Body parts develop with increased usage and weaken with disuse

56. What does it mean when someone says that electric charge is conserved?

a. Like charges repel, and unlike charges attract.
b. The net charge of an isolated system remains constant.
c. Charges come from electrons and protons.
d. Charge can never be created or destroyed.

57. The air passing over an airplane's wing is considered an irrotational fluid flow. Which of the following statements correctly describes the concept of irrotational fluid flow?

a. The fluid flows in a straight line.
b. All particles have the same velocity as they pass a particular point.
c. A tiny paddle wheel placed in the fluid will rotate.
d. The fluid does not have any rotating points, whirlpools, or eddies.

58. Which of the following is considered observational evidence in support of the Big Bang Theory?

a. Expansion in the redshifts of galaxies
b. Measurements of cosmic microwave background radiation
c. Measurements of the distribution of quasars and galaxies
d. All of the above

59. What type of change occurs when a liquid transitions to a gas?

a. A phase change
b. A chemical change
c. Sublimation
d. Condensation

60. The distance from the earth to the sun is equal to which of the following?

a. One astronomical unit
b. One light-year
c. One parsec
d. One arcsecond

61. Substance A has a density of $5.0\ \text{kg/m}^3$ and substance B has a density of $4.0\ \text{kg/m}^3$. What is the ratio of volume A to volume B when the masses of the two substances are equal?

a. 1.25
b. 0.80
c. 1.12
d. 0.89

62. Which of the following is an example of an absolute age?

a. A fossil is 37 million years old.
b. A rock is less than 100,000 years old.
c. An organic artifact is between 5,000 and 10,000 years old.
d. All of the above

63. Which of the following statements correctly describes an effect of the Gulf Stream?

a. It increases humidity along North America's west coast.
b. It makes the climate of South America colder.
c. It makes the climate of Northern Europe warmer.
d. It makes the climate of the Caribbean milder and less humid.

64. A cube of aluminum is placed at the bottom of a deep ocean where the pressure is over 20 atmospheres. What happens to the density of the cube?

a. It remains the same.
b. It decreases slightly.
c. It increases slightly.
d. It becomes zero.

65. Which of the following is needed for an experiment to be considered successful?

a. A reasonable hypothesis
b. A well-written lab report
c. Data that others can reproduce
d. Computer-aided statistical analysis

66. Which of the following is an example of a density-dependent limiting factor?

a. Air pollution by a factory
b. The toxic effect of waste products
c. Nearby volcanic eruptions
d. Frosts

67. Which simple machine was used to raise this flag?

a. Screw
b. Pulley
c. Lever
d. Inclined plane

68. In which of the following scenarios is Mario not applying work to a book?

a. Mario moves a book from the floor to the top shelf of a bookcase
b. Mario lets go of a book that he is holding so that it falls to the floor
c. Mario pushes a box of books across the room
d. Mario balances a book on his head and walks across the room

69. Once a hypothesis has been verified and accepted, it becomes which of the following?

a. A fact
b. A law
c. A conclusion
d. A theory

70. Why is it more difficult to push a shopping cart full of groceries than an empty shopping cart?

a. The full cart has less mass than the empty cart
b. The full cart has a greater mass than the empty cart
c. The full cart has less friction than the empty cart
d. The empty cart is not pulled down by gravity

71. Which of the following materials has randomly aligned dipoles?

a. A non-magnetic substance
b. An electromagnet
c. A permanent magnet
d. A horseshoe magnet

72. Which of the following conditions would promote evolutionary change?

a. Random mating
b. A large population
c. An isolated population
d. Gene flow

73. Thermohaline circulation is caused by:

a. Temperature differences between seawater only
b. Salinity differences between seawater only
c. Variations in seawater density caused by both temperature and salinity differences
d. None of the above

74. The first living cells on earth were most likely

a. Heterotrophs
b. Autotrophs
c. Aerobic
d. Eukaryotes

Refer to the following for question 75:

Your 9th grade biology class is about to take on its first animal dissection. You have already covered the procedure in detail during class, but you know that some of the students are still feeling nervous or even a little queasy.

75. Which of the following procedures would be INCORRECT regarding dissection?

a. The specimen should be rinsed before handling.
b. Harmful chemicals should be disposed of according to district regulations.
c. Decaying specimens are never permitted.
d. Students with open sores on their hands that cannot be covered should be excused from the dissection.

76. A student is working on a science project and is going through each step of the scientific method. After the student conducts his or her first experiment and records the results of the experimental test, what should the student do next?

a. Communicate the results.
b. Draw a conclusion.
c. Repeat the experiment.
d. Create a hypothesis.

77. In humans, more than one gene contributes to the trait of hair color. What is this an example of

a. Pleiotropy
b. Polygenic inheritance
c. Codominance
d. Linkage

78. Which of the following demographic changes would lead to a population with an older age composition?

a. Increased birth rate
b. Environmental pollution
c. Increased availability of food
d. Medical advancements that increase life expectancy

79. In birds, gastrulation occurs along the

a. Dorsal lip of the embryo
b. Embryonic disc
c. Primitive streak
d. Circular blastopore

80. When students are taught science, the information needs to be:

a. Correct, contextualized, and explained
b. Diverse, multicultural, and functional
c. Demonstrated, teacher-prepared, and manipulative
d. Theoretical, practical, and researched

Answer Key and Explanations for Test #2

1. A: In a Zn-Cu battery, the zinc terminal has a higher concentration of electrons than the copper terminal, so there is a potential difference between the locations of the two terminals. This is a form of electrical energy brought about by the chemical interactions between the metals and the electrolyte the battery uses. Creating a circuit and causing a current to flow will transform the electrical energy into heat energy, mechanical energy, or another form of electrical energy, depending on the devices in the circuit. A generator transforms mechanical energy into electrical energy, and a transformer changes the electrical properties of a form of electrical energy.

2. B: Phyletic gradualism is the view that evolution occurs at a more or less constant rate. Contrary to this view, punctuated equilibrium holds that evolutionary history consists of long periods of stasis punctuated by geologically short periods of evolution. This theory predicts that there will be few fossils revealing intermediate stages of evolution, whereas phyletic gradualism views the lack of intermediate-stage fossils as a deficit in the fossil record that will resolve when enough specimens are collected.

3. D: *Genetic engineering* is a general term to describe altering DNA sequences through adding or removing pieces of DNA from a native sequence. In the earliest genetic engineering processes, restriction enzymes were used to perform this "clipping" function, but other methods have been devised and are in use today. Current technologies include those using nucleases (such as CRISPR-Cas9, zinc-finger nucleases, or TALENs) or site-specific recombinases.

4. C: This is indeed a systematic error and must be treated accordingly. Answer A is probably not realistic in that the student may not be qualified to recalibrate the instrument. Answer B is incorrect as the scientific process does not include ignoring errors and assuming they are minor. Answer D is also incorrect as it is not random and does not take into account that the collected data will be off by 0.7 degrees.

5. A: Homeostasis involves the balancing of many biochemical systems and process. Several of them include buffers as a means of expanding the range of stable conditions. In this instance, part of blood pH maintenance is controlled with the carbonic acid, H_2CO_3, and bicarbonate ion, HCO_3^-, buffer. While water, even when neutral, has a small amount of hydronium ions $(H_3O)^+$and hydroxide ions, OH^-, present, they do not act as a buffer (B). Electroplating copper onto tin is a redox reaction (C). The lack of solubility of aluminum hydroxide does not make it a buffer (D).

6. C: According to Hardy-Weinberg equilibrium, $p + q = 1$ and $p^2 + 2pq + q^2 = 1$. In this scenario, $q^2 = 0.25$, so $q = 0.5$, and p must also be 0.5.

7. A: When light waves hit a convex lens, they are refracted and converge. A convex lens curves or bulges with the middle being thicker and the edges thinner. A magnifying glass is an example. Light rays are refracted by different amounts as they pass through the lens. After light rays pass through, they converge at a point called the focus. An object viewed with a magnifying glass looks bigger because the lens bends the rays inward. Choice B would indicate a concave lens as it would cause the light to be refracted and diverge. Light is not reflected in this case, so neither choice C nor D would be applicable.

8. A: Solutions and compounds used in labs may be hazardous according to state and local regulatory agencies and should be treated with appropriate precaution. Emptying the solutions into the sink and rinsing with warm water and soap does not take into account the hazards associated with a specific solution in terms of vapors or interactions with water, soap, and waste piping systems. Ensuring the solutions are secured in closed containers and throwing them away may allow toxic chemicals into landfills and subsequently into freshwater systems. Storing the solutions in a secured, dry place for later use is incorrect, as chemicals should not be reused due to the possibility of contamination.

9. D: Two genes next to each other (or within a specified close distance) are said to be linked. Linked genes do not follow the law of independent assortment because they are too close together to be segregated from each other in meiosis.

10. D: Biomass pyramids are graphical representations of the total amount of organic matter present within an ecosystem. Most terrestrial ecosystems have the traditional pyramid presentation with the smallest point at the top. In aquatic ecosystems however, the pyramid is often inverted with the major producer within the system having a smaller biomass than the consumers above it. This is generally because the producers, often phytoplankton in these cases, produce multiple generations quickly while having shorter individual lives. These are then quickly devoured by the substantially larger mass of zooplankton.

11. B: Concerning answer A, if an object has a positive charge, it is because electrons were removed. In the case of a conductor, the electrons will migrate away from the surface, leaving a positive charge on the surface. The electric field of a negative point charge points towards the charge. The electric field of a sheet of charges will be perpendicular to the sheet.

12. D: Mercury is a fat-soluble pollutant and can be stored in body tissues. Animals higher up the food chain, which eat other animals, are most likely to accumulate mercury in their bodies.

13. C: Prokaryotes, or simple cells that lack a nucleus, appeared on Earth approximately 3.8 billion years ago. Eukaryotes, or complex cells, emerged 2 billion years ago, and arthropods developed about 570 million years ago. Amphibians emerged approximately 360 million years ago.

14. D: The frequency of ocean waves is measured by the number of wave crests that pass a given point each second. The crest of a wave is its highest point, and the trough is its lowest point. The horizontal distance between two subsequent crests is called wavelength, and the height is the vertical distance between a single wave's trough and crest.

15. A: The relationship between wavelength and frequency is inversely proportional, and in general, the speed of sound is constant for almost all frequencies. So, the relationship between all three is defined to be: frequency times wavelength is equal to the speed of sound in a given medium, or $f \times \lambda = v$.

16. A: Pioneer species colonize vacant habitats, and the first such species in a habitat demonstrate primary succession. Succession on rock or lava often begins with lichens. Lichens need very little organic material and can erode rock into soil to provide a growth substrate for other organisms.

17. A: Chemical compounds are formed when valence electrons from atoms of two different elements are shared or transferred. Valence electrons are the electrons located in the outermost shell of the atom, and they occupy the highest energy level. Atoms may form compounds by sharing valence electrons (covalent bonding) or by transferring electrons.

18. A: Redshift is observed when a light-emitting object moves away from an observer. The observation of cosmological redshift supports the notion that the universe is expanding and the distance between Earth and distant galaxies is increasing. Redshift is an increase in the wavelength of light that appears visually as a movement toward the "red" end of the spectrum.

19. A: Since change in velocity divided by change in time equals acceleration, the slope of each line segment on this graph represents acceleration. Line segments I and IV both have zero slope, meaning there is no change in velocity over the time represented. No change in velocity means the velocity is constant. Therefore, lines I and IV represent constant speed.

20. C: All line segments on this graph represent acceleration since velocity divided by time equals acceleration. The line with the steepest slope represents the greatest acceleration. The steepest line is V, so option C is the correct answer.

21. C: Disruptive selection occurs when the environment favors alleles for extreme traits. In the example, seasonal changes can make different types of food available at different times of the year, favoring the large or small bills.

22. A: Active and passive learning are the two general categories of learning.

23. B: The electrolysis of water is a chemical change that transforms water into hydrogen and oxygen gases. Synthesis reactions are those that combine reactants to form a product, which is the opposite of what happens when electrolyzing water. Reverse osmosis is a technique often used to purify water by forcing impure water through a semipermeable membrane using a pressure differential.

24. B: An iron bar moving inside a coil of wire that contains a current would create an electromagnet. Rapidly spinning and rotating electrons inside an iron bar (A) creates a magnetic field. The movement of electrons through a complete circuit (C) is an electric current. Convection currents within the liquid core of Earth's interior (D) create the Earth's magnetic field.

25. B: Secondary succession occurs when a habitat has been entirely or partially disturbed or destroyed by abandonment, burning, storms, etc.

26. A: Vultures eat carrion, or dead animals, so they are considered scavengers. Detritivores are heterotrophs that eat decomposing organic matter such as leaf litter. They are usually small.

27. D: The graph represents a set of data. The line graph increases in distance from 1 second to 4 seconds and then begins decreasing. The only data set that shows distance increasing and then decreasing is set D.

28. B: Kinetic energy is the energy of motion and is defined as $KE = \frac{1}{2}mv^2$. Using this equation, if you double the mass and the velocity of an object, you find $KE = \frac{1}{2}(2m')(2v')^2$, or 8 times the original KE. Therefore, the motorcycle has 8 times as much kinetic energy as the bicycle.

29. C: The mass of the ball is appropriately called a control variable for the experiment. A control or controlled variable is a factor that could be varied, but for testing purposes should remain the same throughout all experiments; otherwise, it could affect the results. In this case, if the mass of the ball was changed, it could also affect the length of the period. The length of the string is meant to be an independent variable, one that is changed during experiments to observe the results upon the dependent variable, which is the variable (or variables) that are affected. In this case, the period would be the dependent variable.

30. A: A formalized hypothesis written in the form of an if/then statement can then be tested. A statement may make a prediction or imply a cause/effect relationship, but that does not necessarily make it a good hypothesis. In this example, the student could rewrite the statement in the form of an if/then statement such as, "If the length of the string of the pendulum is varied, then the time it takes the ball to make one complete period changes." This hypothesis is testable, and doesn't simply make a prediction or a conclusion. The validity of the hypothesis can then be supported or disproved by experimentation and observation.

31. B: Work is defined as the force used to move a mass over a distance. The amount of energy used to accomplish a job is a non-scientific definition of work. The amount of energy used per unit of time is the definition of power. Energy stored in an object due to its position is the definition of potential energy.

32. D: Smallpox is the only disease that has been eradicated by immunization. Progress has been made in the elimination of measles, mumps, and polio.

33. C: A physical change occurs when water condenses. The only thing formed during condensation is new intermolecular bonds. Therefore, no new covalent bonds form (B). The only time new atoms form is during a nuclear reaction (A). The water molecule is not ionizing, so no new ionic bonds form (D).

34. A: Experiments are conducted in order to test a hypothesis. Collecting data (B), identifying a control state (C), and choosing variables (D) are steps in conducting an experiment designed to test a hypothesis.

35. A: The table shows a clear correlation between mass and jump height. If you put the list of jumpers in order from highest mass to lowest mass, they will also be in order from highest jump height to lowest jump height. Choice D can be eliminated immediately because there is no information about any of the individuals' heights in the data table or in the question.

36. A: A calorimeter is used to measure changes in heat. This instrument uses a thermometer to measure the amount of energy necessary to increase the temperature of water.

37. D: The field of stratigraphy is divided into several subfields, each of which focuses on a unique aspect of sedimentary material and yields unique insights about the material's age. In the subfield of chronostratigraphy, a material's age is estimated by determining when it was formed or deposited. The study of the vertical layering of rock types is called lithostratigraphy, and the study of fossil ages in rock layers is called biostratigraphy. Magnetostratigraphy examines data about changes in detrital remanent magnetism (DRM) at the time rocks were formed.

38. A: When an external force deforms a solid material, it will return to its initial position when the force is removed. This is called elasticity and is exhibited by springs. If too much force is applied and the elastic limit is exceeded, the rod won't return to its original shape any longer. As with springs, the deformation is directly proportional to the stress. The elastic limit occurs in rods subjected to a tensile force when the strain stops being directly proportional to the stress. The typical pattern when the force increases is that the strain increases linearly, then it doesn't increase as much, and then it breaks.

39. B: It is true that galaxies are gravitationally bound, so that structures within them orbit around the center. Galaxies do contain dark matter, and only the largest "giant" galaxies contain over one trillion stars. The smallest "dwarf" galaxies contain as few as 10 million stars. Clusters and superclusters are composed of many galaxies.

40. C: In the field of geology, the term "uniformitarianism" refers to the belief that the natural forces, laws, and processes that shape the Earth have remained relatively constant over geologic time. This belief contradicts catastrophism, which maintains that dramatic events have been the primary forces involved in shaping the Earth.

41. C: Wheel A is turning clockwise, which causes wheel B to turn counterclockwise. Wheel B then causes wheel C to turn clockwise. Wheel C in turn, turns wheel D in the counterclockwise direction. The question states that the wheels are in contact, and the number of intermediate wheels does not prevent the turning motion from being transferred all the way down the line.

42. D: Covalent bonds form when two nonmetals bond. Oxygen (O) is the only nonmetal in the answer choices. Iron (Fe) is a transition metal. Lithium (Li) is an alkali metal. Argon (Ar) is a noble gas and does not react with other elements.

43. C: Jabir Ibn Hayyan, Antoine Lavoisier, Dmitri Mendeleev, and Marie Curie are associated with the study of chemistry. Isaac Newton, Albert Einstein, Richard Feynman, and Stephen Hawking are associated with the study of physics. Robert Hooke, Louis Pasteur, James Watson & Francis Crick, and François Jacob & Jacques Monod are associated with the study of biology. James Hutton, Charles Darwin, Georges Cuvier, and Alfred Wegener are associated with the study of geology.

44. A: The appearance of the Coriolis effect in the Earth's oceans is caused by the Earth's rotation. The Coriolis effect results when free objects such as water move over a rotating surface such as the Earth. As water moves from the poles towards the equator, it curves slightly westward, while water moving in the opposite direction (from the equator towards the poles) moves slightly eastward.

45. B: Since the ammeter is connected in series, it will draw current and reduce the current in the resistor. However, ammeters have a very small resistance so as to draw as little current as possible. That way, measuring the current doesn't significantly affect the amount of current traveling through a circuit. Voltmeters, on the other hand, are connected in parallel and have a high resistance.

46. C: It is true that subsurface currents are driven by temperature and density variations, while surface currents are driven by wind. Ocean currents affect vast quantities of seawater and strongly influence the climate of Earth's landmasses.

47. A: When using a light microscope, total magnification is determined by multiplying the ocular lens power times the objective being used. The term "ocular lens" refers to the eyepiece, which has one magnification strength, typically 10x. The objective lens also has a magnification strength, often 4x, 10x, 40x, or 100x. Using a 10x eyepiece with the 4x objective lens will give a magnification strength of 40x. Using a 10x eyepiece with the 100x objective lens will give a magnification strength of 1,000x. The shorter lens is the lesser magnification; the longer lens is the greater magnification.

48. B: When the accumulation of snow and ice exceeds ablation, a glacier will gradually form. Ablation is the sloughing off of ice and snow through melting, evaporation, sublimation, and wind erosion. When snow and ice accumulate faster than ablation occurs, a glacier will form and continue to gain mass until the rate of ablation overtakes the rate of accumulation.

49. B: The two slits cause the light beams to diffract, that is, spread out instead of traveling in a straight line. As a result, there are two light beams superimposed on one another. When the two light beams constructively interfere, there are bright lines, and when the two light beams destructively interfere, there are dark lines. A chromatic aberration has to do with blurring through a lens due to different colors of light. Doppler shift affects the wavelength of light from moving sources. Total internal reflection is 100% reflection of light at the boundary between certain materials.

50. B: Carbon is released in the form of CO_2 through respiration, burning, and decomposition.

51. D: Within a habitat, there is a maximum number of individuals that can continue to thrive, known as the habitat's carrying capacity. When the population size approaches this number, population growth will stop.

52. C: The Cosmological Principle is best described as a working assumption that has testable structural consequences. The principle, which underlies existing cosmological theories, assumes that the view of the universe possessed by observers on Earth is not distorted by their observational location. The observable implications of this theory are homogeneity (the same types of observational evidence are available regardless of one's vantage point within the universe) and isotropy (the same observational evidence is available by looking in any given direction from a single vantage point).

53. C: The state of matter in which atoms have the strongest bond is the solid state. Matter, which is defined as any substance that has mass and occupies space, can exist as a solid, liquid, gas, or plasma. The atoms or molecules that form solids possess the strongest bonds, while those that form plasma possess the weakest bonds.

54. B: Fission occurs when the nucleus breaks up into two smaller nuclei. When certain nuclear isotopes absorb a neutron, they become unstable and split, starting the process of fission. The average binding energy per nucleon increases with a fission reaction, and the two new nuclei are more stable than the initial nucleus. The increase in binding energy comes from the changes in mass of the protons and neutrons (note: both protons and neutrons are nucleons). The release of energy is part of the fission reaction, but this does not explain why the fission reaction occurs.

55. D: Natural selection was Darwin's idea, not Lamarck's. Mendel discovered that genes are the basic units of inheritance. Lamarck's observation about use and disuse is true, although he did not connect it with the underlying mechanism of natural selection.

56. B: Although like charges do repel, and unlike charges do attract, the question is indirectly asking about the law of conservation of charge. In other words, when someone mentions electric charge being conserved, they are saying the net charge of system remains constant. Charge originates from electrons and protons is only partially true because there are other elementary particles with charge. Charge can be created or destroyed because a photon will produce an electron-positron pair. There is also the example of a proton and electron combining to form a neutron.

57. D: Irrotational fluid flow consists of streamlines, which describe the paths taken by the fluid elements. The streamlines don't have to be straight lines because the pipe may be curved. Answer B describes the conditions for steady flow. The image of a paddle wheel may be used to explain irrotational flow, but (1) the wheel will not turn in an irrotational fluid flow, and (2) this only works if the viscosity is zero. When there is viscosity, the speed of the fluid near the surface of the pipe is less than the speed of the fluid in the center of the pipe. Rotational flow includes vortex motion, whirlpools, and eddies.

58. D: Expansion in the redshifts of galaxies, measurements of cosmic microwave background radiation, and measurements of the distribution of quasars and galaxies are all considered observational evidence in support of the Big Bang Theory. The abundance of certain "primordial elements" is also consistent with the theory.

59. A: The addition of energy causes a phase change. Phase changes are physical changes, not chemical changes. While sublimation is an example of a phase change, it occurs when a solid turns directly into a gas without passing through the liquid state. Condensation, another phase change, occurs when a gas turns to liquid.

60. A: The average distance from the earth to the sun is equal to one astronomical unit (AU). An AU is equal to 93 million miles and is far smaller than a light-year or a parsec. A light-year is defined as the distance light can travel in a vacuum in one year, and is equal to roughly 63,241 AU. A parsec is the parallax of one arcsecond and is equal to 2.0626×10^5 astronomical units.

61. B: The density of a homogeneous object, liquid, or gas is its mass divided by its volume, or the ratio of its mass to its volume. Density is inversely proportional to the volume and directly proportional to the mass. The ratio of the density of A to the density of B is $5:4$ or $\frac{5}{4}$. Hence, the ratio of the volume of A to the volume of B is $4:5$ or $\frac{4}{5}$. Alternatively, one could solve the equation $5V_A = 4V_B$.

62. A: When a fossil is determined to be 37 million years old, this is an example of an absolute age. Absolute dating, which can be accomplished through the use of radiometric techniques, establishes precise ages for materials, while stratigraphic techniques only produce relative dates. Relative dating can establish approximate ages for rocks and fossils based on clues in the surrounding rock, but it cannot be used to determine absolute age.

63. C: The Gulf Stream, which is a surface current that originates in the Gulf of Mexico and travels across the Atlantic Ocean, makes the climate of Northern Europe warmer. After traveling up the eastern coast of the US, the Gulf Stream splits into two forks. The North Atlantic Drift travels across the ocean to warm Europe, while the southern fork travels toward West Africa.

64. C: In a vacuum, the only forces acting on the molecules of aluminum are other aluminum molecules. Inside a fluid, the molecules of the fluid collide with the sides of the cube and exert a force on the surface causing the cube to shrink in size slightly. Also, the temperature of water deep in the ocean is very low. This causes the vibratory motion of the aluminum molecules to decrease, which decreases the dimensions of the cube.

65. C: For an experiment to be considered successful, it must yield data that others can reproduce. A reasonable hypothesis (A) may be considered part of a well-designed experiment. A well-written lab report (B) and computer-aided statistical analysis (D) may be considered part of an experiment that is reported on by individuals with expertise.

66. B: Density-dependent limiting factors on population growth are factors that vary with population density. Pollution from a factory, volcanic eruptions, frosts, and fires do not vary as a function of population size. Waste products, however, increase with population density and could limit further population increases.

67. B: Pulley. A pulley is a simple machine that has a wheel with a rope wrapped around it. The flag is attached to the rope, which is pulled to raise the flag. Therefore, the correct choice is B.

68. B: When Mario lets go of the book, he is no longer exerting any force on it, so he cannot be doing work on it. In all the other examples, Mario is exerting a force on the book in the direction that it is moving. In Answer A, Mario moves a book from the floor to the top shelf. Mario lifted up vertically on the book, in the same direction that the book moved, so he was doing work. In Answer C, Mario pushes a box of books across the room. This is also an example of work being done because the box moved in the direction of the force Mario applied. In Answer D, Mario is indirectly applying a horizontal force to the book because of the friction between the book and his head, so he is exerting a force on the book in the direction he is moving.

69. D: Once a hypothesis has been verified and accepted, it becomes a theory. A theory is a generally accepted explanation that has been highly developed and tested. A theory can explain data and be expected to predict outcomes of tests. A fact is considered to be an objective and verifiable observation, whereas a scientific theory is a greater body of accepted knowledge, principles, or relationships that might explain a fact. A law is an explanation of events for which the outcome is always the same. A conclusion is more of an opinion and could be based on observation, evidence, fact, laws, or even beliefs.

70. B: The empty shopping cart does not weigh very much and is easy to push. As groceries are added to the empty cart, the cart gains mass. By the time the shopping cart is full, it has more mass than it began with and requires more force to push it.

71. A: Magnetic poles occur in pairs known as magnetic dipoles. Individual atoms can be considered magnetic dipoles due to the spin and rotation of the electrons in the atoms. When the dipoles are aligned, the material is magnetic. Choices B, C, and D are all magnetic materials. Therefore, the magnetic dipoles in these materials are not randomly aligned. Only choice A has randomly aligned dipoles.

72. D: Random mating (A) or a large (B) or isolated (C) population describe conditions that would lead to genetic equilibrium, where no evolution would occur. Gene flow, which is the introduction or removal of alleles from a population, would allow natural selection to work and could promote evolutionary change.

73. C: Thermohaline circulation is caused by variations in seawater density caused by both temperature and salinity differences. This process, which affects subsurface ocean currents, contributes to the mixing of seawater and accounts for the relative uniformity of the water's physical and chemical properties.

74. A: The first living organisms probably had not yet evolved the ability to synthesize their own organic molecules for food. They were probably heterotrophs that consumed nutrition from the "organic soup."

75. C: When performing a dissection in class, decaying specimens can be permitted under certain circumstances, but unknown specimens are never permitted. Rinsing the specimen before handling can help wash away excess preservative, which may be irritating. Disposing of harmful chemicals according to district regulations is always required. Excusing students with open sores on their hands that cannot be covered is a good precaution. Exposure to pathogens and toxic chemicals can occur through open breaks in the skin.

76. C: Repeating the experiment validates data. Each separate experiment is called a repetition. It should be possible to replicate the results of experiments or tests. Similar data gathered from many experiments can also be used to quantify the validity of the hypothesis. Repeating the experiments allows the student to observe variation in the results. Variation in data can be caused by a variety of errors or may be evidence against the hypothesis. Answer D, create a hypothesis, comes before experiments. Answer A, communicate the results, and B, draw a conclusion, occur after testing.

77. B: When more than one gene contributes to a trait, inheritance of that trait is said to be polygenic. This type of inheritance does not follow the rules of Mendelian genetics. Pleiotropy is the opposite, which one gene contributes to two or more unrelated traits. Codominace is a non-Mendelian inheritance where both alleles are expressed in a heterozygote individual, rather than the dominant allele being expressed and the recessive being masked. Gene linkage occurs between two genes that are located near each other on a chromosome and are usually inherited together.

78. D: Prolonging the life of individuals in a current population will lead to an older age composition. An increased birth rate will cause population growth, but a greater proportion will be younger, not older.

79. C: In birds, the invagination of gastrulation occurs along a line called the primitive streak. Cells migrate to the primitive streak, and the embryo becomes elongated.

80. A: When students are taught science, the information needs to be correct, contextualized, and explained.